Love Cartography by Lisa Fabrega

Published by Lisa Fabrega International, LLC

Tampa, FL 33634

www.lisafabrega.com

Cover and Design by Angela Hammersmith

Photos by Lisa Fabrega unless otherwise noted in photo.

Edited by Marybeth Bonfiglio

ISBN-13: 978-1987706420

First edition

• NOTE FROM THE AUTHOR •

This is a book in the style of biomythography. Biomythography is a term and style of writing created by the writer, Audre Lorde. It is often characterized by combining myth, biography and history in narrative or poetic form. This style of writing allows for the writer's unique perception of events, places, people and incidents she experienced to be represented in their re-telling. I have changed names, characters, places, identities and incidents in order to protect privacies.

As is common in poetry, many characters, situations and perspectives through which experiences are shared are also entirely fictional, as poets often write from the perspective of fictional characters to recreate a mood or an experience. Any resemblances to actual persons, living or dead, businesses, companies, events, or locales is entirely coincidental.

Any conversations recreated in this book come from my memory and should not be mistaken for word-for-word transcripts or perfectly recollected, exact retellings. Memory mixed with emotions can be a one-sided thing in that they can be subjective to a person's individual experience, so anything written here should not be taken as the absolute truth about any situation represented here. There are, of course, always many sides to a story and I do not wish to tell someone else's story or experience for them. I can only tell my own.

All perspectives and points of view represented in this book are mine alone and do not represent anyone else's. Some experiences mentioned are an artistic combination of personal myth and actual facts and should not be taken to be exact records or verifiable occurrences. Stories and experiences have been re-told in my way in order to preserve the personal lensing through which they were experienced.

• TABLE OF CONTENTS •

III. THINGS THAT MADE US

IV. LOVE, SEX, DESIRE

V. RISING

• FOREWORD •

"Planets in the 9th and 10th houses!" she exclaimed.
"You are an explorer!"

"But not only of the earthly landscapes."

The astrologer winked at me with a spark in her eye on that last sentence, implying I knew what she meant. And I did.

For as long as I can remember I have had a hunger in me to know everything about the world. That includes insects, animals, strange phenomena and people. I want to know what makes things the way they are, what makes people tick, why we make the choices that we do, what are the names of things.

When I was a child, I used to get in trouble for asking too many questions. For knowing too much for my age. I devoured books at the rate of 5 per week. I read the age-appropriate books my mother got for me at the library, but I also snuck from her library *The Joy Of Sex*, *The House Of The Spirits* and several books by Swami Muktananda.

It wasn't just knowledge for knowledge's sake that I was seeking. It was understanding.

As an adult, I have traveled a lot. This hunger has driven me to explore countries where the language is melodic and strange to my ears, where the scents are familiar or where the customs are alien to my own. I make trips locally all the time to the undiscovered places locals take for granted. Sleeping in a hostel or in a luxury hotel, it's no different to me. Each trip is its own new experience. Each mountain, each story, each positive or negative experience brings me face to face with an unknown part of myself.

Traveling has made me realize how connected everything and everyone truly is. But I don't travel for the glamour of it or for the perfect photo to show off to other people. I travel because I want to know what lies outside of me. What is outside of my own limited perspective that I have yet to learn? What lies in the unknown that we fear to enter? What other marvelous thing is there to learn that may never have crossed my awareness had I remained in the same place?

People are countries, too.

When I meet people I feel drawn to, I want to know everything about them. I want to know their deepest secrets, the intimate things about them that no one else knows. And in fact, I often find myself in conversations where people feel the desire to share these things with me. Maybe they can sense my explorer's hunger and feel safe. Maybe it makes them feel deeply loved that someone would care to know all of the intricate details that make them who they are.

What I have discovered in the last 39 years is that there are many different kinds of landscapes.

There are the astounding, alien-like glaciers of Iceland and the rainforests of Panama. The lavender fields of France and wine-infused hip movements of people walking down the streets in the small towns of Italy.

Those are earthly landscapes. And there is much to learn from them, if we dare to leave our comforts and have the humility to learn from that which is unknown.

And there are landscapes not only of this earth,
but of the heart and the soul.

People are landscapes. There are entire oceans of feeling and countries of thought inside of them, if you take the time to approach with the same wonder as you would a waterfall.

Moments in our lives are undiscovered towns sometimes named Disappointment, Grief or Lust.

So, yes, I am a lifelong explorer. Of all landscapes. And to be an explorer of life and love… that feels particularly poignant in this day and age, when it seems like the fabric of society might be falling apart and increasingly the unknown goes from being powerful teacher to instead the fearful "other."

What if we all looked through the lens of the explorer? What landscapes might we see that we had never seen before? What new textures and languages might inform the very cells of our being and change us positively, forever?

A lot of people told me not to release this book. They think it's not smart for *this* to be my first book.

The "marketing formulas" say the first book for an "expert" such as myself must be a how-to, a listicle, a personal development step by step tome. I'll write one of those soon, too.

But a book filled with photography, poetry and secrets *is* a personal development book.

This book is its own continent.
A new landscape for you to step into.
A landscape of love, looked at from the different lenses and perspectives from which the narrator speaks. Even the photos, which I've taken in my explorations of daily life around the world, are their own worlds.

I named this book "Love Cartography" because this book is about discovering the landscape of love that lies within each one of us.

That is my hope for you as you read the book. That you will learn something new about yourself looking through these different lenses. That something aslumber will awaken. Or that you'll remember something important about yourself.

And I believe that in the end, so much of what we are looking for is love.
We are love, we came from love and we are always trying to get back to love.

Each section of this book is divided into different countries of feeling and experiences. Three to be exact.
You will find yourself moving through varying landscapes of emotion and thought.
Let it all happen to you. Do not be afraid of what might come up.

I highly recommend savoring each piece slowly and deliberately, like you would the hip curve of a new lover or a rare, delicious fruit you've just discovered in a new land.

These days everyone tells writers "write tiny bite-sized pieces because no one has time and everyone's attention span is short."

But rushing through a country and only stopping for the cheap thrill tourist spots is about the worst way to travel. You'll never get a feel for the rich life of a new place that way, nor will you ever know its true soul. You will only have the experience as viewed through the limits of your own perspective, instead of experiencing a place for what it actually is.

My favorite experiences of travel, and one I often try to replicate in the retreats I lead as part of my business, are the ones where you have no perfect plan and where no tourists go. Those always end up being the most magical experiences. And the ones that grow us the most.

The same goes for your life.

Rushing through your life, never allowing yourself to slow down and really enjoy the way a work of art has the power to change you or invite you to think and create differently… never stopping to experience the things that require the unfurling of time (like a sunset, a hummingbird drinking from a flower or a nice, long orgasm) is no way to truly live a life.

When you get reduced to being nothing but a short attention span, you become just a reaction to the world around you, instead of a fully fleshed person with a multitude of beautiful things to share and experience. This is why we sometimes get so far from ourselves and feel like we've lost the soul of who we are. And we wonder how we can get it all back.

It's starts with giving ourselves the space to slow down, feel and experience how life wants to move through us.

So, approach this book as you would a luscious destination. With curiosity, excitement, maybe a little reverence and a willingness to be changed by it, forever.

Use this book as your tool to slow down, savor, be present and *feel* in a world that is always inviting you to rush and put yourself last.

Pick a piece per day and write in your journal about it.
Share with me on social media what it brought up for you or share with a loved one in your life.

This book is about mapping the vast internal and external landscapes of the heart, the soul and the human experience, through the lens of a love cartographer.

This is about *you* becoming a love cartographer.

For many years, maps have allowed humans to navigate and understand complex landscapes and situations. Maps are what allow us to have some direction and not go totally blind into the unknown. Maps support spacious behavior, spacious problem solving or simply more awareness of the space around us. Maps allow us to remember where we found that amazing restaurant in the middle of nowhere. The mountain on which we had our first broken heart. The stream by which you decided to finally choose yourself.

Without cartography, we wouldn't have maps and without maps, we would not know how far we have come, where we still want to go. Without maps we don't have the information we need to make good decisions in the unknown lands of life.

May this book be the map to undiscovered parts of you, or places within you that you have not visited for a long while, but long for. May you find yourself staring back at you in these pages and may you fall in love with the complex beauty of the vast landscapes that lie within.

With love,

Lisa Fahrega

• ABOUT THE AUTHOR •

Photo by Wendy K Yalom

Lisa Fabrega is the founder and CEO of Lisa Fabrega International, a company created for big-vision, high achieving women leaders who are here to leave legacies in the world. She is the creator of the Empress Circle (a mastermind for high impact women leaders who are ready to create their legacy footprint in the world), Soul Adventures (retreats for high performing women to sacred global sites to reconnect with the soul voice) and The 7 Soul Gates (a 12 week experience for leaders to clear blind spots, elevate impact & connect to intuition).

Lisa was born in Panama and grew up in the dictatorship of Manuel Noriega. The removal of basic rights of speech deeply impacted her at the age of 10. After her family adopted two boys from the ghetto and one died and the other ended up in jail, despite a mountain of support from her parents, her heart was broken. She became obsessed with what it is that makes some of us overcome, while others cannot. She has dedicated her life to helping others overcome their internal obstacles so that they can create legacies in the world.

Her heroes are numerous, but most influential to her are bell hooks, Audre Lorde, Charlotte Bronte, Martin Luther King, Oprah, Mother Teresa and Amanda Palmer. Lisa is a citizen of the world, but spends a lot of time in her favorite place in the world, Santa Barbara, California where you can find her meditating in the garden most mornings, writing, coaching clients and laughing at the everyday antics of all the birds that live in the trees above her. If she's not there, you'll find her spending time with her sister's children, whom she basically considers her own, too.

Her biggest goals in life are to travel to space, learn 5 languages (she currently speaks 3 fluently), be interviewed by Oprah under her two favorite oak trees and become her bestie, have a love that will be spoken about for ages, write 6 books & travel to as many countries as possible before she dies.

Though she is a master coach who regularly sells out her private coaching and masterminds, she considers herself above all an artist and a writer. Her weekly, truth-telling and vulnerable writings about her life and challenges as a leader have inspired tens of thousands of women for over 8 years and her programs have changed thousands of lives.

You can sign up for her emails or explore other ways to work with her at LisaFabrega.com. You can find her on Facebook and Instagram (where she regularly posts funny, interesting videos about her life and thoughts) as well. Simply search for her name.

I

WHAT IS PROMISED

A prayer for precarious times

I.

I am floating in the middle of the ocean.
It's 1:22 pm on a Thursday.
I am thinking to myself how vast this feels
how this feels like exactly what I am supposed to be doing.
In this state of salty suspension I am brainless.
This is unsettling.

I try to reach for thoughts.
They don't come.
I am the waves rocking.
A limitless pool of fish and wet wildlife unseen.
The lap of the Mother.
I am exactly where I need to be.

This is not a fully relaxed state.
Part of me wants to get out of the water.
Guaranteed safety.
Be in air conditioning. On a soft couch.
A place where nothing happens.

II.

This is the Pacific ocean. Green and murky.
I can't see what is at my feet.
I can't see what might be coming towards me.
I imagine what a bite and a tug would feel like.
My feet land on something hard and sharp buried in the sand.

I don't like the unknown power of the ocean.
You cannot predict how she will use it.

She is a lovely, untamed force.
A woman unto her own.

I am that woman.
We are that woman.
With crusted bits of salt and dried up pieces of seaweed in her hair.

And yes, this is exactly where I need to be.
Forcing that small part of me to surrender.
To be batted around by the waves.

I watch them gathering towards the horizon.
They grow and grow towards me, an ominous invitation.

I feel the tightening of my stomach as I unravel the part of me that
knows *anything could happen when that wave gets to me*.

I could die. I could drown. I could completely let go.

When it finally reaches me, it gently lifts me up and places me back
down, but I am never in the same position I was in. Always I am facing
a different direction

Legs twisted. Arms struggling to catch their balance.

Deep calm and wild fear all at once.
She places me in position,
preparing me for the next wave.

III.

There is no one on the beach today.
Yesterday I was in this exact spot and there was a family.
Three children, a husband and wife playing right next to me.
I watched the kids running head first into the huge crashing
waves, getting completely beat up, twisted and turned, salt
water up their noses and sand in their bathing suits. They were
screaming with excitement and I laughed and played in the
water just like them.

But today is not the same.
Yesterday the ocean was playful. Today she smells different.
She isn't sure if she wants to be menacing or nurturing.

Like me.

IV.

I saw a movie today about a woman who travels to the most beautiful places in the world for a living. She always travels alone, but sometimes she meets interesting men and wonders, *should her life have been different?*

Her family doesn't understand what she's done.
How could she choose this and be happy?

They think she is lost. Thrown her life away.
A woman who has wandered into the ocean on purpose with nothing to keep her afloat.
Is this madness?

But the movie ends with her getting on a plane to the next horizon, fulfillment spread out across her face.

I feel like someone has made a movie about me.

An ancient pain blooms in my chest, as old as my memory of the sea.

It is true that freedom will always separate you from those who birthed you, in the end.
This calling towards vastness,
it comes with a price.

In my head a poem begins to form and a big wave catches me, tumbles me upside down into a soundless landscape.
Lost again. Alone. Smiling as the chaos roars.

V.

At the bottom, with my face pressed against the sand and broken bits of seashells violently batting around my ears, I surrender.

There is nothing to do but this.

When I surface, the next wave hits me and this time, I invite her.
I invite her to pull all of the poison out of me.
Pull all that is not me, away, away, away.

Pull all that encumbers us and makes us small, back into her abyss.
Please, leave us clear, full of stars and tourmaline. Amen.

I say this prayer fervently as my head goes underwater again
and the next giant wave washes over me.
I say it for myself and for all.

And suddenly I understand how to get out of the ocean.

I move forward towards the sand when the waves push me there.
I stop when she draws back in upon herself and wait.
When the next wave comes, I let her rock me towards the shore.
Little by little until I am finally on all fours.
Wet. Trembling. Panting for air. On the sand.

Ready to walk.

Photo by Kym Pham

That which you savor on your tongue

There are secret desires that murmur.
Soft round things, innocent and bright.

They have been there within you
for centuries. And I have watched you

rolling them back and forth
across your tongue,
afraid to savor.

Let yourself be led by
that spark of hot desire.

Let it pull you gently
into new lands.

Stop it with the *practical*.

Freedom is your undoneness,
even when your knees
tremble.

Psalm of all things

I remember when we went out into the trees
at dawn not caring
about the strange-looking wet patches
the grass would leave on our jeans.

At the river bank you asked me to sit
and feel
the woods around me.
Like a master enforcing his pupil
into a sacred
silence.

I didn't have the heart to tell you
I'd been doing this since I could first breathe.

What I knew
was that
there is no true
silence.

The world
gives off a hum that starts low
and then deafening.

That if you listen close
you can hear within you
the very molecules of leaves
singing.

And I remember your face
as I sang you the song
that has no name
and how you finally
got it.

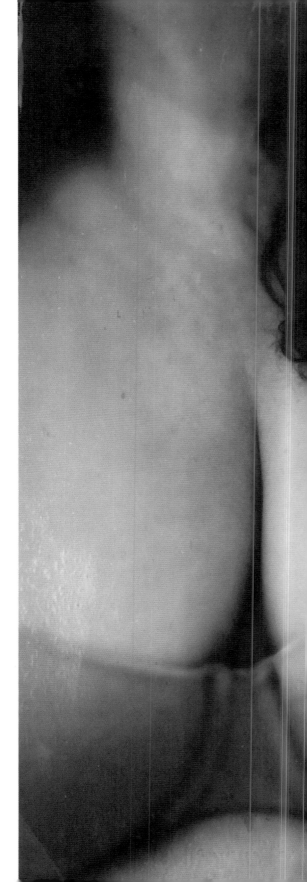

How I learned to be a woman

He pushed her down
in between the flowers
and the tree she had been
longing to climb for two weeks.

Even though she had just beat him twice
in arm wrestling, with his hand on her
down there she was too stunned to move.

And there was that moment.
You know the one.
Where time no longer exists
and a breath can't be counted.

She could hear all the other kids
playing and screaming in the background.
And here she was, being *put in her place*.

She could not read his eyes.
Whether he was weighing something worse
or feeling that innocent part of him dying.

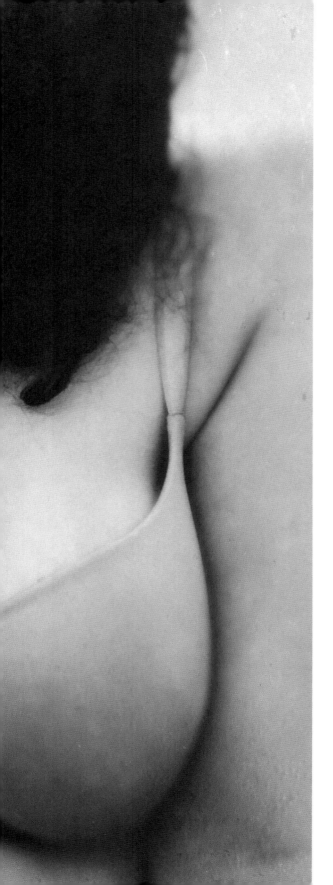

Because there is something in you
that perishes when you violate
or overpower.

She could hear the ants
crawling in the grass beneath her ears.
His ragged breath.
Her heart trying to escape
through her teeth.

Then he was gone.

This is the story she
waited twenty eight years
to share with her daughters.

This is how I learned
what it is to be
a woman.

Ode To Desire

I love it when my longing meets your longing.
That I can be consumed by you
while you're elsewhere in the world
writing
walking the dog
crossing the street
unaware.

I love the way my breath constricts
in a small
short
gasp
everytime I think of you
standing near me,
demanding everything.

I think this must be the way a person
takes their last breath,
A hot thrill of final
surrender
shooting through their spine.
I love how you smile when you know
that I want you to push
up against my resistance.
That my shadow
turns you on.

I love that I hold your darkness
inside of me as much as your light.
That it rubs me the wrong way,
Makes me push you away,
pulls me in, repels me
fascinates me.

I love that there will always be more

more places within me,
you,
that we don't want each other
to discover,

as we invite each other
in.

The things of which you secretly dream

some days you wake up and your heart
is poetry and you don't know what to
do with all of those sweet storms,
where to put it or who
to speak it to.

so you whisper it into existence,
a prayer that is afraid
to be heard, to sweeten
your lips as it leaves
in small, timid puffs of air, threatening
to take form,
become true.

it's okay to weave sweetness
into the molecules of air
that surround your face.

it's okay to let your heart swell
with the brightness of hope.

you're allowed to keep that fervent idea alive,
like a hot coal in your chest.

sometimes it's the only thing that will
keep you warm when the mind goes dark,
clinical and gray.

get a whiff of your honeyed breath
as you speak your desires
quietly to the bees or shout them
from the wing of a plane
30,000 feet in the air.

You're not here to be liked

You are not here to be liked.

You are here to breathe sacred truth
into the wanting atmosphere.

Play the opposite of safe.

Leap off cliffs,
plunge into the blue waters of unknown

Feel the exhilaration that is on the other side
of what you thought was fear.

Your life is art.

Hold the tender places between your ribs
that say
do not love me.

Rock the boat until the whole damn thing flips over.

Redefine the status of the quo.

Burn down and rise.

Experience longings that are untold.

whisper prayers into the stars and surrender
to the faith
that they are being heard.

Unlock the God within
you.

Liked is complacent.
a comfort you cannot afford.
the slow death of your heart.

Liked is a cage where the cowardly go to die.
a forgetting
of who you Are.

You
are not here
to be liked.

Photo by Wendy K Yalom

Photo by Kym Pham

Revolution

It is a revolution
to simply be a soft place for
you to land.

How to remember to be brave

I am God herself.

Shaped into bone and flesh.

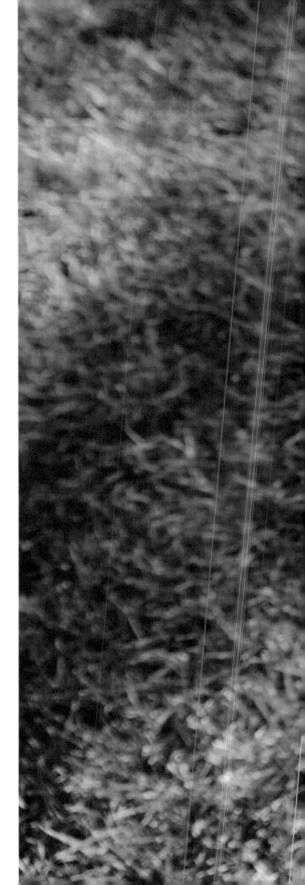

How to love yourself

All of those terrible choices.
All of the
red-in-the-face-when-you-think-of-them
utterances,
the soft pulsating shame
of those vulnerable moments.

You see the reason to shrink,
you shy away from the messiness.

I ask for your wreckage.

In the shrapnel of this secret life that you
push away from you with embarrassment,
I hold the awkward pieces
with a hot, violent sort of love.

This darkness is brilliant.
Necessary, important.

It is the rough-edged,
burnt, twisted-metal Savior
that you've been waiting for.

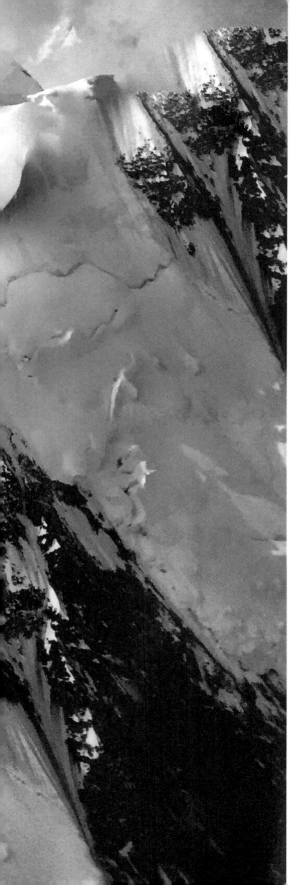

Your heart is the heart of all

Sometimes you get
a sensation
that is the intersection
between cry
laugh
orgasm
love and
leap.

It is a memory
of your original
state.

But you were yanked
into a body in the world
of men

and now you walk around
like an amnesiac, so afraid
of feelings.

But that
sensation
always returns

to remind you
you are the constant hurdling
towards change.

It is written
that your heart
is here to
crack,

your chest
was made to hold
the whole of everything that

ever was.

II

SHADOW
SIDE NOW

Primordial Egg of Atomic Desire

"Just as life gestates in the egg, so in ancient healing rituals would initiates withdraw into a dark cave or hole to "incubate" until a healing dream released them reborn into the upper world, in the same way the chick crawls out of the egg. Alchemy depicted the germ of the egg contained in the yolk as the "sun-point," the infinitesimally small, invisible "dot" from which all being has its origin. It is also the creative "fire-point" within ourselves, the "soul in the midpoint of the heart," the quintessence of golden germ" that is set in motion by the hen's warmth "of our devoted attention"

— The Book of Symbols —

It's been 2 weeks since Lucy died.

Time heals all wounds, she says. I wonder if that's true.
Maybe there are some wounds that always feel as fresh as the day they were born.
Maybe 'healing' is only getting distracted from the wound more easily over time.

It's been 2 months since I began this transition.

I pulled a card from the deck, cicadas buzzing.

The Queen of Death.

You cannot cheat death.
You cannot outrun her.
You can only ride the River Styx in her skirts of surrender.

The Black Queen is with me.
In the shape of a vulture she has walked
beside me with a pomegranate in her hand,
the sickly intoxicating scent of jasmine pours from her eyes,
fixed straight on me, drawing a five-pointed star on my heart.

In the beginning, the god Chronos placed seeds within five corners of the earth. From these corners the cosmos appeared. Out of pure Desire.

I was preparing to speak to a room full of women about Desire.

In my meditation, the white owl handed me this key,
"you are the keeper of the primordial flame," she said.

In the beginning, there was the void.
In the beginning, there was blackness.
In the beginning the Creator lay fallow and empty, reclined.
And from her longing sprung the seed.

The seed sprung from Desire.
And the seed grew and multiplied.

All of creation sprung from the fallow lap of nothing.
All of creation sprung from Primordial Desire.

The seed is Desire.
Desire sprung open the seed.

I think of the seed. I think of the egg.
Which came first, the seed or Desire?

Inside that tiny hole, inside that yolk of incubation there is the bright point of longing. There is the orange flame of desire, germinating.
From this tiny dot of light comes all of life.

At the center of the atom, there is a tiny dot of energy, so powerful that when released it can obliterate an entire city, country, planet.
This miniscule spot of illumination has, since the beginning of time, destroyed planets and from their ashen bones and carcasses new stars have come to life.

The Queen of Destruction, she places the open pomegranate in my hands,
she says 'think of what it takes for the seed to become life, for the egg to crack
open into a living, dangly-limbed thing…

Of course you're tired.'

I've just experienced a loss.
They tell me I shouldn't be alone right now.
They tell me I am supposed to distract myself.

But I remember this from a Book of Symbols I read a long time ago:

"Alchemy depicted the germ of the egg contained in the yolk as the "sun-point," the infinitesimally small, invisible "dot" from which all being has its origin… [this point of light] is set in motion by the hen's warmth "of our devoted attention."

"Think of what it takes for the seed to become life, the egg to crack open into a living, dangly-limbed thing…"

A complete turning inside.
Turning the great eye of our attention inward, to the center point of the egg.
All energy must be saved for the process of the nucleus bursting forth into life, light.

Think of the energy it takes for the living being inside the egg to crack open the shell and take its first breath in its new form.

"All of your energy must be reserved for this process," she says.

My brain has stopped working. "I cannot access my brain," I tell her.
I'm having trouble making sense of what it is that I'm supposed to do.
"I'm on the brink of something huge, something huge and I need to figure it out."

Now is not the time, she says.

> *Now is not the time.*
> *Now is the time to become the egg.*
> *Now is the time to lie, suspended and reclined.*

It is winter. It is the eve before the New Year.
Everything is barren and twigs.
The ground is hard and fallow.

In the beginning, the Creator lay there, reclined and fallow.

Now is not the time for pushing, or birthing.
Now is not the time for yellow bursts of energy or
solar flares of Sun.

Now is the time for black holes and dark matter.
Now is the time for Ereshkigal to hang you up in the underworld,
naked and heaving on her meat hook, your rotting mixing in with
the scent of the jasmine laced around your neck.

It's been 2 weeks since I was seized with an uncontrollable urge for pomegranate seeds.

I brought them home, anomalies in this obscenely fertile third world country of mangos and papayas. I held both of them in my hands, gently carving the seeds out, swallowing them whole, while the blood red juice ran down my chin and stained the corners of my mouth.

I could not get enough,
watching my belly grow,
full of pomegranate seeds.

If you were to enter a black hole, within seconds you'd be ripped apart and there would be nothing of you left. But the most amazing thing is, the rate at which you are ripped apart is so intense, that the very act of your destruction emanates light.

For your heart, awaiting the sun

I

These mornings,
when the heart
wakes up
raw
and trembling,
are not for
wild
savages of
feeling.

They are not
for those who cut
through jungles
with machetes and pick-
axe, venturing forth,
bold.

They are
for those who sit
in silence, awaiting
the sun.

They are
for those who have
surrendered
everything.

They are
for those whose hurt
is still
tender
and encircled.

II

Let the world
witness you, naked
like a child who doesn't
know what to do
with all of the life
rushing
through her.

There is nothing

to do except
sit
patiently,
wide-eyed
and bare,
allowing
the sunlit ocean to
turn your eyes
all sparkling
and blue.

What the sea returns

I prayed fervently to the sea
yesterday, standing knee deep
in its murky green lap, cupping

in my hand the tiny, white seashell
I'd rescued moments before,
with half of her body buried
in the thick volcanic sand.

I couldn't help it. My heart
was swelling and she looked
so small and pure. Enough
to hold the sadness of a woman
filled with storms.

Enough to sanctify the ardent
longings I whispered into the smooth curve
of her back.

A stranger passing by in that moment
surely saw a wild-haired woman singing
preciously to the small hole in her curled hand,
flinging the things that are wanted but cannot
be spoken into the waves, arms stiff

with the wildest hope.

The year that God stopped speaking

You didn't answer my prayers,
so I turned to moonlight
and the tiny creaking frogs
that came back to the canyon
after four years of drought.

You stopped speaking,
so I let the spiders weave whispers
around my ears to catch insects
that would tell me Everything.

You only showed me the void into which
all of my entreaties disappeared,
so I went outside every night
and turned to black holes.
I let them rip me open, limb by limb
until all that was left of me was light.

For when you forget to use your lungs

there are days
when the only words
that come are
hold on.

And you repeat it
over and
over and
over to yourself
like a mantra
that reminds you to
use your lungs.

Hold on

Hold on

Hold on.

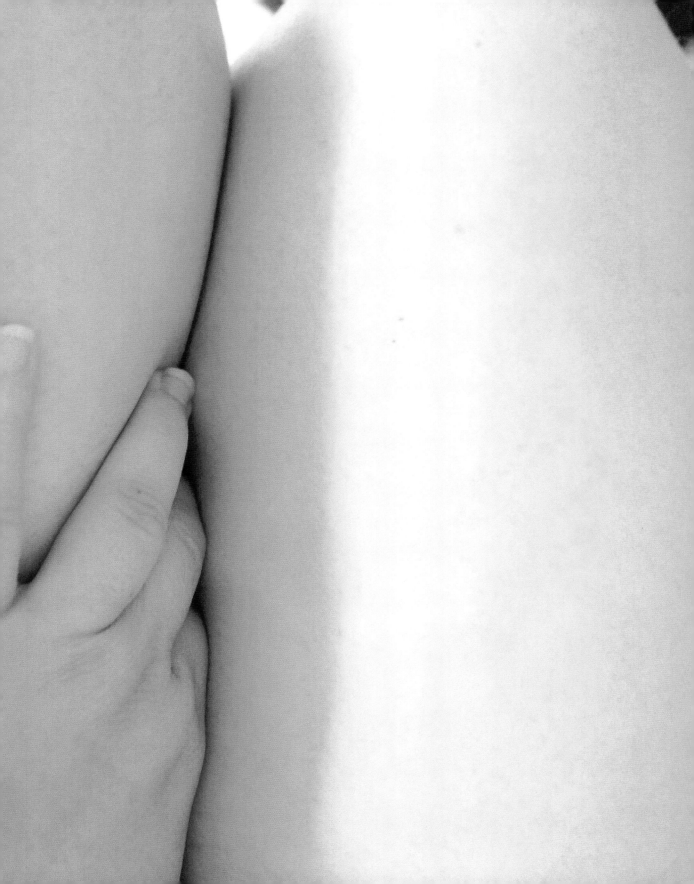

I am my own widow

In the darkness
something nameless is birthed.
An unconscious thing

You go to bed feeling one way,
the next thing you know,
there is a new creature
sitting on your lap at dawn.

She is misshapen and mysterious,
glass-like. She is soft and liquid
to the touch. She demands you turn
in upon yourself and cloak.

She teaches you all about the things that lurk
between the shadows, the silence between
synapses, the space between your ribs.

She shows you
a new way to sing.

And then, there you are,
all slick and shiny with your
afterbirth.

With your heart suddenly as open
as the sky.

Baptism

The sages say longing
is the most sacred emotion.

I lay in my bed, every night
experiencing the sacred. Consumed
by this peculiar desire
to be obliterated, licked
head to toe by its
blue flame.

How many have lain here
like me, under peeling ceilings,
thatched roofs, comets and
bright stars.

Centuries of longing
threads weaving together the palms
of all of these empty hands.

The saints and mystics had ecstasy.
I am almost certain this is the same.
Here is the impossible union.
Baptismal waters that give birth to this
exhilarated pain.
Among the whirling planets is my
religion,

all aflame.

Of Comets

It's always like this.
A growling despair
In the dark right before I birth
you.

It starts small,
with a pang of yearning

and ends
in consumption.

This is what it means
to be art, combustible.
My desire is flammable.

This is what it means
to be of comets,
inflamed bodies carrying
the eons of mankind's longing,
around the Great
Sun. The way some god
must have longed for us

before he lit the match.

On longing

The places where we long to be met by another
are the places where we long to meet ourselves.

All longing
is longing
for lost parts
of the Self.

How I learned to believe in magic

You ask me
to tell you
what I remember
I say:

I feel
I've just been
through a 39 year
war.

And I am
just now taking
my first full breath
free from gunpowder.

I am
just now removing
the last bits of shrapnel
my mother lodged
inside my lungs
long ago.

I am like most survivors:
my memories are selective.

A person doesn't have time
for moments
when they are always
just praying to survive
with their heart still whole.

You tell me
there is violence in your chart.

But when it happened,
you couldn't speak.
you would just
implode.

Yes

but have you ever felt
what it is to swallow
the magma of humiliation?

Have you ever had your soul
beaten out of your body
because you spilled some milk
reaching across the table
for the last scraps of love?

Have you ever replaced your ears
with the sound of trees
to forget the sizzle of a leather belt
burning through
your skin?

You tell me
this has always
made me question
if I really deserve
the good things
that come to me.

But I remind you
I am done
being the nuclear reactor
for the pain of foreigners.

I am done
drawing myself down
from standing on the shoulders
of women who only birthed me
to be their wound.

I am finally removing
the skin of this profound loss
from my heart.

I say to you:
do you know
I only recently realized
that I have never really felt
loved? Like,
down-to-the-bones-love.

I am just now learning
there are arms that exist
free from land mines,
where a woman
can finally rest.

I am done imploding.

And I am here now.
For all of it.

…

This is how I learned to believe in magic.

Because I had to look for it.

When I feel alone

The wind knows your name
in case you should ever forget
and need it whispered back to you
syllable by syllable.

The morning knows your soul,
should you ever lose it
and need it gently carried back to you
as you open your eyes.

If you ever feel lonely, know
that everything desires you

and everything dead remembers you.

Sometimes I stay away from oceans.

Sometimes I stay away from windows
overlooking scenic panoramas.

I don't trust myself to remember
that I can't fly

Sometimes I stay away from piano concertos.
I might forget I have a body, that I'm not just
a soul that can be beautifully played.

Sometimes I stay away from mountains.
I might remember
and ecstatically disintegrate
when there is still so much
to do,
be, love,
still.

Poem For The New Year

This morning the prevailing topic
at breakfast is: *there is nothing new
left.*

Try telling that to the sky, I think,
or the wild blue wind. Each morning
there is something new,
my eyes confess to it.

Every second of the day
two hundred thousand leaves
on a tree are changing
to a different shade of green
under the pompous sun, flagrantly
flaring in patterns unfathomable
and unknown until this
very millisecond.

Try telling that to the heart,
every day discovering new
profundities.

Everything is new.
And nothing is.
It's your choice.

Surrender

Tell me.
Yesterday in the languid
afternoon heat,
did you surprise yourself
with your own ardor?

Did you marvel at the
imperceptible breach in breath
as beauty dripped from the world
and on to your engulfed heart?

Did you buckle under the white
weight of your unquenched
thirst?

Did you catch yourself waiting
to surrender?

Let go.

Let the world announce you
into her great song,
weaving you over and over
into the deep heart

of all things.

Photo by GeneticBo

Photo by Kym Pham

Birthright

Know this:

it is your birthright,
to be loved all the way down
to the part of you that is so vast
you become an empty space

filled with atoms and unknown magic.

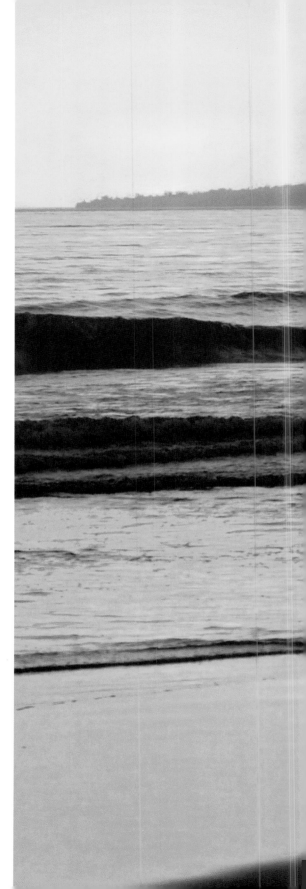

What it means to have a mission

Carry a passion
for something so hot
it leaves a blue hole
in the center of your chest.

Willingly throw your heart away
into the horizon, every day, hoping
that it will be of service,
the kindling to someone's spark.

Derive ecstasy from this sacrifice,
lay your body in the pyre
of humanity as an offering.

It is way beyond me, this pull.
It transcends want, desire
and ego.

It devours sleep,
incinerates all that does not
prostrate before it.

It requires sword,
blood and ceremonial
feathers.

It requires doubt,
fear and blindness.

It asks me to open softly to terror,
surrender to that which is
dark and unholy.

Doubt that there was ever anything
good inside of me while ghouls
scream in my ears and all
becomes ash. And then

Reincarnate as a mantle of stars,
red-feathered bird
rising.

I prayed and no one answered

Sometimes it takes not having prayers answered
to understand the true meaning of faith.

Sometimes you have to feel the fear
that arises when no one is there,
to understand the unending presence
of unconditional love.

Sometimes you need to feel the void
into which prayers disappear
to finally believe in your own magic.

In your ability to answer prayers
for yourself.

Watching clouds in Florida

Can we ever fully see a person
without sewing a piece of ourselves
onto them?

I lay on the wet morning grass,
feeling the slippery bodies of snails
taking their time across my palms.

I let the sun burn me in between
the eyebrows and turn me within.

And that is when I See.

On Seeing (Cherry Blossom)

I am a purveyor
of emotions.
I deal in feelings
and meaning
and the way my godson's eyes
resembled liquid metal
the first time he discovered
humor.

It is a curse.
to see
what most people won't.
To notice
the way your grandmother's shoulders
hunch over when she catches
your grandfather's scent lingering
on his favorite chair years after his death.

And then there's yesterday afternoon.
Where I stood, heart blooming
while the wind whispered its gifts
to me, under the pink veil
of a blossomed cherry tree.
Perfumed
and unfurling into the miracle
of the next. In these moments

I am glad I See.

How to own your power

You don't need to
own your power.

You are power.

I am a mountain

I am not made of stones
only jagged pebbles honed
for centuries by the deep sea.

I am not feathered or soft,
my body yields to suppleness.

I am not delicate, I am gentle.

I am not fearless, I am a mountain,
resilient and deliberate, carving devotion
into the redolent shoulder of the wind.

I am not a volcano, I am a century of
desire, burning.

I am the ash, rich in memory.
Molten.

Yearning.

Photo by Wendy K Yalom

III

THINGS THAT
MADE US

Rainstorm, Steenhatchie, 1997
(Watching my grandfather die)

You brought death to the thunder.
To think on it now, the two of us
at your bedside, communicating
through synapses.

How could it not have been the time for you to go?
The moments then seemed so important.
Unplanned, miraculous. The ticking clock
so inherent to the state of our hearts. Meanwhile,

the mind
on rolling clouds, large shafts of light.
The air in our lungs at four a.m.,
calling owls, crouching low with the gun.

I know now that you planned it this way.
All the while in that hospital room,
our bodies becoming meaningless,
distracted by the fear of your death.

And your hands, those hands,
shaping and stretching our souls out
over the lands that you loved,
out through the skies
and the thick marshy air.

Now, at four a.m, I stand here
frozen-still, five feet from a doe.
I see in her eyes
what you had planned for us

all along.

Oregon

We both
pulled over to take photos
of the way those trees cast their shadows
across the open field.

Those are the kinds of things you see
and think no one could ever notice
with the same awe.

But for three seconds our eyes met
and you nodded. As if to say
in the history of the entire world,
there will never be another moment like this

and we are the only two who will know.

Panamanian Diner

In the steam room yesterday,
on the wet, iridescent bench,
sprung a fountain of smooth sadness
from my chest,
all bubbling and blue.

In the blind air, I tried to feel
around for what it was or
give it a name, like: *this is the hurt*
from my mother or
this is from the look he gave me,
even though he was
in love with someone else.

But this was a new kind of sadness,
effervescent and pure.
And it had no name.
When it went away
seconds later I thought, *well that's*
that. But it came back that afternoon,
while having a pineapple juice with my friend
in the Panamanian diner. I told her about it.

How I could almost savor its
undiluted-ness, how sometimes
I see how we are all just ants.

We talked about the first time we each realized
that there is no meaning. How there are pockets
of life, whole worlds in each human being
sitting next to us that we will never even
know.

I never found a name for this
wellspring of melancholy that has been
spurting forth from my heart at random
intervals since. But I notice how my heart
can feel absolutely demolished
and elated all at once, when I sit
at this counter and watch the men
make sandwiches so skillfully, as if
this is what they've been waiting to do

all of their lives.

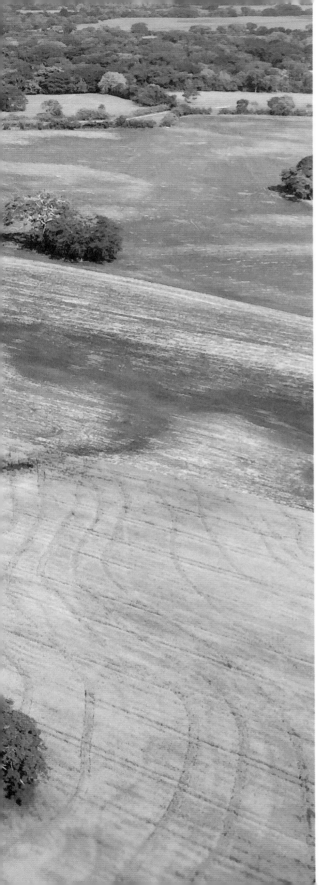

For the lonely man who travels

I'd like to be told
just once, that
I can stop running now,
kick off my shoes
without caring where they land.

I'd like to finally be told
that there's a hot meal
waiting for me
on the plastic checkered
table cloth.

I'd like to receive an ecstatic face
after having been gone
instead of a room that must be
emptied
of its silence.

I'd like to take
something for granted
because it's always around,
and suddenly remember
how important it is
in a fit of passion.

I'd like to torture someone
with that 10 minute opera song
that no one else
seems to love.

For devotion
to be prized beyond
all things

just once.

The Forbidden Color

Today I was told
I wore the forbidden color.

Imperial yellow-gold
can make your blood run crimson
in the streets
if you were not informed.

This color is meant for emperors
not train drivers.

It is
the most beautiful
of all colors

the center of everything

I marvel at how
throughout the centuries
a color that symbolizes
freedom
has been so controlled.

The cages we create
by fearing a life
lived bright.

How fearful we are
of the yellow-gold expression
of someone's truth.

I wear
my forbidden
yellow shirt
more frequently now.

Photo by Nicole Casteel

Interlaken (In between two lakes)

There was a band of accordions playing
for someone's birthday.

Couples dancing an old Swiss dance
in the tiny restaurant
tucked into the side of a very old mountain
that had fallen in love with the lake.

She was the center, drinking a beer.
Glowing like a woman who has been truly loved.

The corners of her eyes crinkled with the depth
of one who has loved strong and lived to tell of it.

I wanted to sit close to her and inhale the scent
of her wrinkled linen shirt.
I was sure it would smell of salt and softness.

I wanted her to teach me.

But instead I picked a small yellow flower and
readied it as an offering.

*May I one day be loved so well that my
sleeves are slightly worn from the embrace
of an ardent man.*

*May I one day be surrounded by serenades
that make my eyes glow with a bottomless,
feminine strength.*

*May I be that woman who offers rivers of herself
with an ease that makes everyone dance around her.*

Amen.
Amen.

Amen.

Give Yourself To The World

I am on a plane
writing a living will
and the thought
slips in unannounced.

All that I have built
and no one to leave it
to. This little dent in the world
that I've relentlessly carved like
the wind does a mountain,

patiently and with ardent devotion.

Like a captor scratching her way
through a four foot thick cement
wall, mad for freedom
and life.

I want to feel sorry for myself or
find an excuse to try on
a cascade of self-indulgent loneliness.
But suddenly we are flying
over the ocean and everything
is blue and shining
and I remember again who
I really am, surrendering
my molecules over and over
to the brilliant shafts

of light.

When I'm hurt

When I'm hurt,
the pain shooting
through my spine with its
irreverent heat,

I think

how strikingly similar it is
to the way my body shudders
to receive the inevitable expansion
of pleasure.

When you hurt
me, I refuse
to close. Instead,

I sleep naked for days
laugh heartily
in between cries,
whisper prayers
of deepest gratitude.

I am so glad to be broken open.
I am so glad to feel it all.
It is a privilege
to feel more,
love more,
hand my soft heart
over to my one true
love,

Life.

IV

LOVE, SEX,
DESIRE

Before Love

Before love comes
the greatest darkness.
Howling demons
rattle relentlessly inside you.
And you doubt
anything soft
could ever land.

Before love you are
the ocean at night,
full of danger and
blind bliss. You are
dark matter.
Rough.
Unseen.

You are a supplicant
of longing, a pilgrim
to ecstasy, cracked
open in your evening bed.
A consumed saint.

Before love you are
slumberous,
guarded by a wild thing
with dirty mane and sharp
nails, keening savagely against
doors that will only open
on their own terms.

And then one day, you arise
all honeyed and wet. You are
in love with the molecules
of air. You are in love with
the sensuality of your obscurity.

You are in love with the dark
and disgusting. You are
muddied rivulets of delight.

And love comes.

I love you more

I love you more
within music
especially bells
laid over ambient
hollow sounds.

I always find you there
in between reverb
and echoes.

I love you more
in the red warmth
of a hard tropical sun.
Your scent is that color,
lingering orange even
when I close my eyes.

I love you more
in the blades of grass
that shoot between my fingers
when I grab a handful
of your earth.
Upside down
holding on to your axis
for dear life.

I love you more
when the sky is blue
with possibility or gray
with comfort.
When I fly
to meet you in clouds, day
or night, over the city.

I love you more
when I drive home alone
in my car and echo
with that kind of silence
that makes you realize
that nothing exists,
that you are the bringer
of meaning and light,

that this whole, teeming world
is the song
living itself out
through your red,
vibrating
heart.

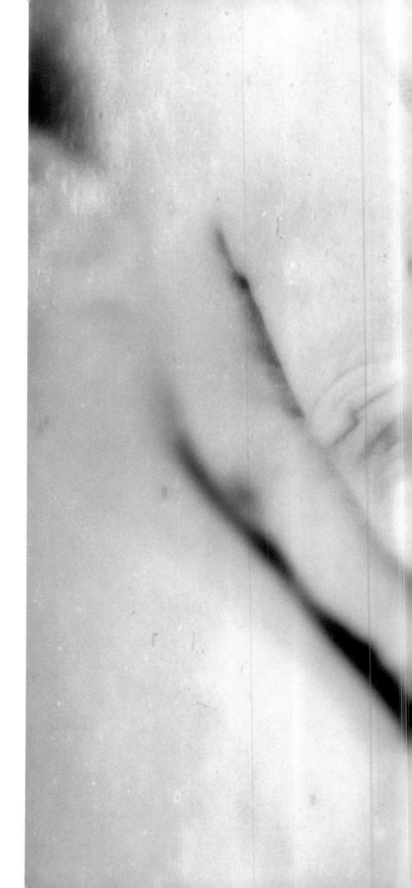

The hidden things

And then I said to him,
*it's the hidden things in you
that I find most*

beautiful.

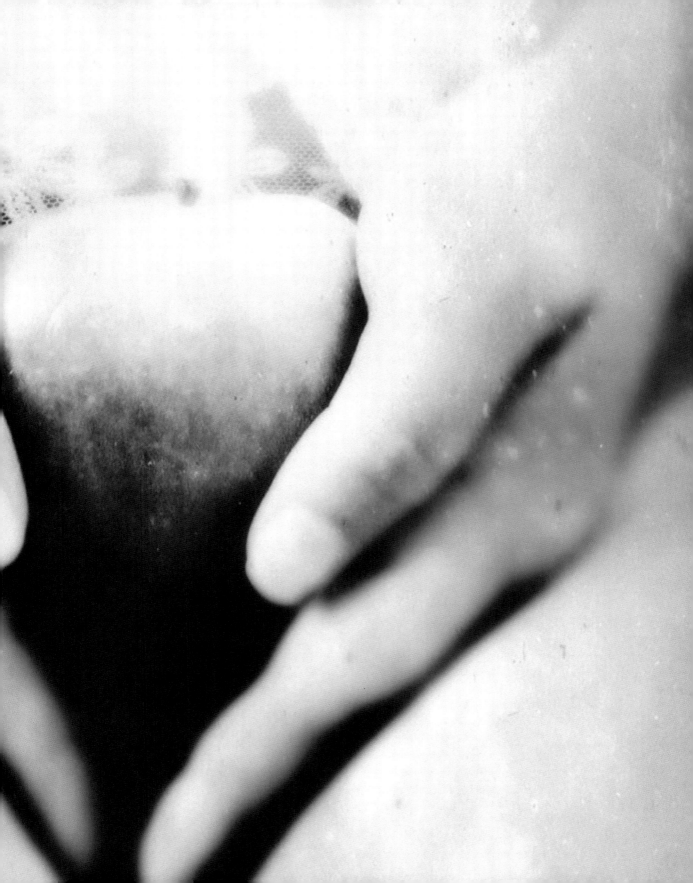

Tricked

Tricked, I walked to the ocean today,
mistaking it for a blanket of stars.
I expected ascendance,
transcendence,
belief.

Instead rivulets
of disappointed foam formed
eddies around my toes, making
my body come alive in all the wrong ways,
switched on by the grotesque and
unexpected.

I stood there for a long time,
cold water licking my heels,
a dead lover beckoning
the warmth of my soft, beating
heart.

I waited.
Caving in on myself with longing
like a woman who waits for her love
to return from the bottom of the sea.
Contemplating surrender
emotionless unknown,
lonely from the grief.

I plunged my face into a cold wave,
expecting starfish, shells, little crabs
and creatures, the sun, stars,
you.

I found the empty stillness of all things,
instead.

All afternoon, I've carried it inside me,
its strange song howling
into the fire in the space
between my breasts.

What I say to you

If you are to love me
you must understand
my love
can never be
Owned.

What pours forth from
Heart onto lips
was meant to fall
on you but also
onto the rest of what is
and what is not.

In my belly
I hold
waterfalls
stars
oceans teeming full
of fish and
depths unknown

all of the atmosphere

dark mountains
that howl into the wind
at night when no one
is listening

comets full of stone
and fire
replicating single-celled
organisms

atoms
leaves
and branches.

My heart holds
all of everything and nothing that ever was,
the loud roar of
the eternal silence
in the spaces between
things that do not touch

longing at the core
of every living
thing.

All things rotting
and coming to life

all things turbulent
and clear.

All things broken-hearted
and whole

all
that flows

from love.

Let me see you

My heart is hurting today.

I can't discern if it is
from pain or opening,
like creaky hinges
that forgot they once
belonged to beautiful
red doors.

In the end,
whether pain
or opening,
whether fear of having,
losing, deserving,
or being seen,

it is all a trembling
over what love
could do to us.

You don't see
the heart
is an intractable
organ.

It was made
to break,
to be used until
well-worn.

Because those are always
the softest things.

The things that have sustained
oceans of feeling and stone.

Those are the things one can truly love.

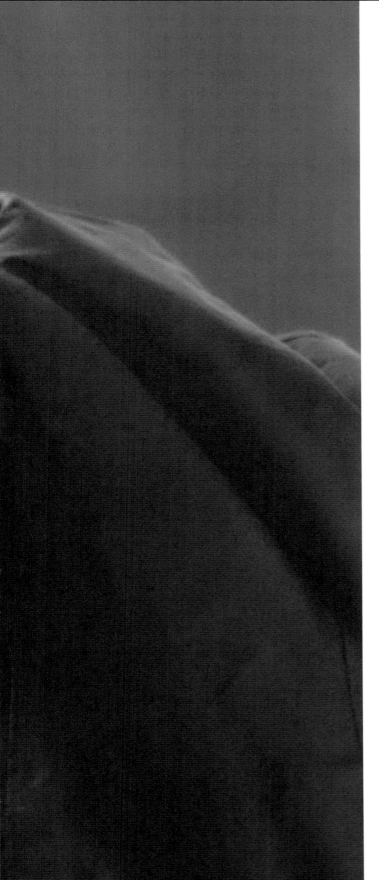

Animal

"There isn't
a single
tattoo
on my body",
I tell you,
proudly.

(I don't tell you that
in the morning
I run my hands
over the soft skin
of my stomach,
breasts and thighs
and imagine they are your hands,
imagine
what it would feel like
to be in your body
while you touch mine)

I use this
tattoo tidbit
to entice you to explore
what you've yet to discover.
Search
every unblemished,
untouched
inch.

In you I want to tease out
the most determined
hunger, the animal
that will never
cease
hunting.

Things too near

Sometimes I want to hold my words close,
guard them like rare seashells in my chest.

There are knowings that feel too precious
to bestow upon anyone who cannot stop
and kneel in awe at their utterances.

There are strings of letters too sacred
to throw into a fire that does not know
the source of its own fuel.

So I warm these words against my flesh,
let them slumber to the soft, steady murmur
of my heart.

There they wait to be given to the one
who walks by with wide enough eyes,
a glistening hunger for the soul of things.

Between Synapses

Let's be quiet
and communicate between
synapses.

Let's touch
and allow only skin
to divulge
what is real.

Swallow me with your eye.

Wake me up in tangles of your
ganglia.

I will kiss them into my heart
until they are no longer heavy.
Blessed by the bright depths
of my love.

Breathe me into your lungs,
make me a whirling dervish of sweetness
perfuming the air you breathe with buoyancy.

Fit me in the palm of your hands
and I will trace my feet along your lines
to show you the map of you.

See what I see.
See why I love you.

Mountains

I came here looking for you
but instead
I found mountains.

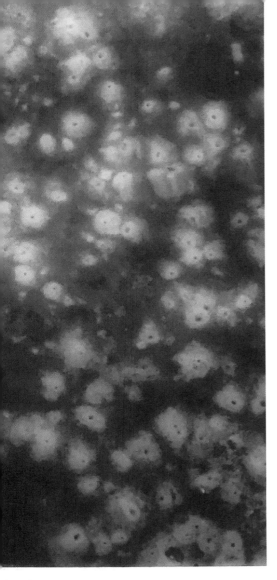

Water

I will meet you
with my whole heart.

I will hold
the full weight of you
In the thin, strong bones
of my ribcage.

I will sit with you in a small room
while you share the things
most cannot hold.

I will answer the phone at 4am
and I will weave your tears
into a blanket of comfort
until you can sleep again.

I will speak with you about
what others have
grown tired of you singing.

I will give you my warmth,
Friendship, a softness you have never known.
I will be a corner you can lean into
with the full weight of your soul.

I will hold your hopes to my chest
as if my own. Dream your dreams
alongside my own.

But mistreat me
a thousand times,
leave me hanging
in the dust. Pretend
that I am invisible.
Betray me. Disappear.
Hand me silent dis-invitation…

The warmth will turn to ice.
I will forget about you.
I will pull those waves of love back
with the force of the tides.

And you will feel it,
though you won't be able
to find the words.

I will disappear
Become a ghost,

back to my liquid depths.

And when you reach out
you will only touch an empty space,
Ice.

This is what it is
to be Water.

Photo by Kym Pham

I want that man

I want that man who
writes poems about
the corners of my mouth.

I want that man who Sees what I already know:

that every piece of me
is made to be worshipped

I want that man who can
lay his heart on my lap without fear.

Not because he is fearless.
But because he knows his heart is bottomless
and never-ending.

I want that man who needs time alone with the land. Not because he is running from himself but because he understands that the wild keeps him breathing.

I want that man
who has no need
to penetrate the space around him
but allows himself
to be penetrated by love itself.

Not because he is without identity,
but because he doesn't need the false safety
of a mask.

I want that man who is the ocean,
vast and ever-present.

Clamoring with music and mystery.

Giving shelter to all that has yet
to be discovered. Space to that
which we will never comprehend.

V

RISING

Morning Prayer

Your voice in me
is the song that is always singing.
Your breath, the prayer
I am always receiving.
Your heart
is my heart--
vast sea
into which
I launch myself
over and over,
infinitely.

Why I hate 6pm

There is a lonesome hollowed out sound of the day dying.

I sit on my balcony as the sun lets the chilled evening pass in front of him. The trees are still bare like exposed human lungs, their bronchi just beginning to give way to brand new shoots of dainty flowers. Pablo Neruda said that at sunset his soul was empty. But mine is not empty, I dread the sunset and I find it terribly lonely.

But it's not empty.

The long, elegant, feminine trees bow to each other, releasing silver rivulets of laughter and off in the distance the long cavernous sound of the ending day gives way to the noise of after-school children playing basketball. It brings back an old yearning, a sick feeling of knowing. That the day is over. That soon, when all is pink, you will have to go back inside and face a slumber that only leads to a dark, heavy expectation of all the responsibilities of the coming morning.

Or the empty feeling of our city-concrete apartments with turquoise walls and tinny marble echoes after coming back from a glorious weekend in the sand, the sun still in between our toes.

A dog howls in the background lamenting the same loneliness that I am feeling. A wind chime lazily gets up the nerve to chime one high note of protest in the absence of the day's warmth.

And here I am.

Not knowing whether to write in this book or look to the sky for that last hope of a bird streaking its way across the sky, bellowing sonancy and smoke.

Neruda is wrong.

It's not empty. It is full.

Full of a beautiful, pink loneliness.

Choose Fire

Laugh until rivulets
run down your legs.

Run towards certain death
with a wide open heart,
giggling.

Lose yourself
in eyes and arms and
scent.

Hurt so deeply you cave in upon yourself.

Turn ashen with rage.
Feel unworthy
unloved, unclaimed.

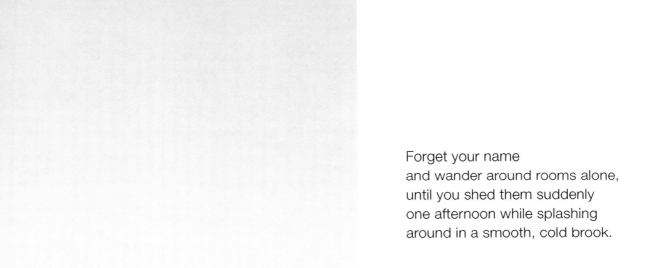

Forget your name
and wander around rooms alone,
until you shed them suddenly
one afternoon while splashing
around in a smooth, cold brook.

Weep in Hawaii as the sun rises
over the volcano while an elder
sings the most beautiful thing
you have ever seen.

Long so ardently you burn yourself
up into pure light.

This is your life.
Choose fire.

Universal Psalm

Even your skin has a song.
It is a song that says
Rise, woman.
Dissolve.

Create the unseen.

Gather your wild psalms
of possibility.
Drink the divine
nectar of this symphony,
disintegrate
every barrier inside of you
until there is nothing but
We.

What all things want to be

You can hold onto pain
until it robs you
of everything, or
you can just
open wider.
Crack
open.
Let it move
through you.
Alchemize
pain
into the ecstasy
that all things
truly want
to Be.

Photo by Kym Pham

• ACKNOWLEDGMENTS •

Thank you to the ones who have broken my heart over and over again. Thank you to the ones who tried to squelch my spirit not understanding how to deal with a young seer girl with a courageous, God-given dedication to her heart. Thank you to the men who inspired many of the love poems, even though in the end you could not see that I was a diamond and you chose to be careless with my heart. Thank you to the friends who have betrayed me and who are no longer a part of my world. Thank you to the ancestors who passed their wounds on to me, leaving it to me to transmute this for the future generations and the world.

I say this not bitterly, I say this with genuine gratitude. For it is you who have hurt me and challenged me, who taught me the power of honoring the self. You have been my greatest teachers. You have taught me to seek more from myself, the world and others. Sometimes we learn most by experiencing what we don't want, so that we can get clear on the deep love and joy that we truly deserve. And this book is a way of leaving those lessons now behind.

Thank you to Marybeth Bonfiglio for being such a wonderful doula for me during this process of putting the writing I had held secretly in a folder for 3 years. Thank you to my sister, Kelly, for cheering me on, and for always being willing to stand at the edge with this deep-feeling, emotional creature who was placed in your life as your older sister. Thank you to my sister's children, Gavino, Henry & Lily for cracking my heart open to a love I have never experienced before. I am honored to be your godmother and I take that role seriously. You are in many of these poems.

Thank you to the amazing clients who have opened their hearts to me and gone THERE with me in so many sessions. Thank you for being so dedicated to leaving a legacy that you would brave these depths of the soul, making sure you don't die with the world having never experienced your revolution. Thank you for recognizing that soul is more important than strategy and asking me to be your guide in becoming a leader of soul in a world filled with ego. You are the changemakers we've been waiting for.

Thank you to the amazing friends who have always seen the higher vision for me and had my back. Dyana Valentine. Jennifer Kem. Tisha Lin. Kym Pham. Samuel Hershberger. Susan Hyatt (who gave me the best birthday celebration ever). Elizabeth Purvis. Breanne Dyck. Selena Soo. Voge Smith. My Aunt Lynn.

Thank you to the lands which have held me, reflected what I needed to know back to me. To the ancestors and unseen guides who have whispered my true name back to me when I have forgotten it. Thank you to the trees for always speaking to me. To the earth for holding me upright when I have felt I had no mother to turn to.

And to Lucy, not just a dog, but the greatest spiritual teacher and love of my life, who sat by my side while many of these poems came to life.

95890892R00164

Made in the USA
Columbia, SC
19 May 2018